FEELINGS

Friendliness

Tamra B. Orr

Published in the United States of America
by Cherry Lake Publishing
Ann Arbor, Michigan
www.cherrylakepublishing.com

Reading Adviser: Marla Conn MS, Ed., Literacy specialist, Read-Ability, Inc.

Photo Credits: © Monkey Business Images/Shutterstock Images, cover, 1, 8;
© Chuck Wagner/Shutterstock Images, 4; © rSnapshotPhotos/Shutterstock
Images, 6; © Sean Locke Photography/Shutterstock Images, 10; © jan_ta_r/
Shutterstock Images, 12; © slobo/iStock Images, 14; © SuzanaMarinkovic/
iStock Images, 16; © Lopolo/Shutterstock Images, 18; ©Stuart Monk/
Shutterstock Images, 20

Library of Congress Cataloging-in-Publication Data
Names: Orr, Tamra, author.
   Title: Friendliness / Tamra B. Orr.
Description: Ann Arbor : Cherry Lake Pub., 2016. | Series: Feelings |
Audience: K to Grade 3. | Includes bibliographical references and index.
Identifiers: LCCN 2015048110| ISBN 9781634710435 (hardcover) | ISBN
9781634711425 (pdf) | ISBN 9781634712415 (pbk.) | ISBN 9781634713405
(ebook)
Subjects: LCSH: Friendship—Juvenile literature.
Classification: LCC BF575.F66 O756 2016 | DDC 177/.62—dc23
LC record available at http://lccn.loc.gov/2015048110

Cherry Lake Publishing would like to acknowledge the work of The Partnership
for 21st Century Learning. Please visit www.p21.org for more information.

Printed in the United States of America
Corporate Graphics

Table of Contents

5   New Neighbors

11 Saying "Welcome"

15 Time for Cookies

19 A New Friend

22 Find Out More

22 Glossary

23 Home and School Connection

24 Index

24 About the Author

New
Neighbors

There is a big truck outside.

It is in front of the **empty** house next door.

Do these people look friendly?

People are getting out. They are carrying boxes.

We have new **neighbors**!

Saying "Welcome"

Can we say hello to them?

We can take over some cookies.

How do you think this girl is feeling?

I want to meet our neighbors.

I want to be friendly. They might have kids my age!

Time for Cookies

We knock on the front door.

They open the door. "Hello!" I shout.

"We brought you some cookies."

Hooray! They **invite** us inside.

A New Friend

I was right. Our new neighbors have kids the same age as I am.

They are **twins**.

How can you tell these boys are friends?

I like them already. I think we are going to be best friends.

Find Out More

Brown, Margaret Wise. *The Friendly Book*. New York: Golden Books, 2012.

Kelly, Mij. *Friendly Day*. Hauppauge, NY: Barron's Educational Series, 2013.

Pfister, Marcus. *The Friendly Monsters*. New York: NorthSouth, 2008.

Snow, Todd. *You Are Friendly*. Oak Park Heights, MN: Maren Green Publishing, 2007.

Glossary

empty (EMP-tee) holding nothing
invite (in-VITE-id) to ask someone to do something
neighbors (NAY-burz) people who live close to you
twins (TWINZ) two siblings born at the same time

Home and School Connection

Use this list of words from the book to help your child become a better reader. Word games and writing activities can help beginning readers reinforce literacy skills.

age	front	neighbors	take
already	getting	new	the
are	going	next	them
best	have	open	there
big	hello	our	they
boxes	hooray	out	think
brought	house	outside	truck
can	inside	over	twins
carrying	invite	people	want
cookies	kids	right	was
door	knock	same	you
empty	like	say	
friendly	meet	shout	
friends	might	some	

Index

boxes, 9

cookies, 11, 17

door, 15

friendly, 13, 21

house, 7

kids, 13

neighbors, 9, 13, 19

truck, 5
twins, 19

About the Author

Tamra Orr has written more than 400 books for young people. The only thing she loves more than writing books is reading them. She lives in beautiful Portland, Oregon, with her husband, four children, dog, and cat. She says that making a new friend is still one of her favorite things to do.